Contents

MATT CHRISTOPHER

On the Court with...

Lisa Leslie

Chapter One

The Girl Who Hated Basketball

"Why don't you play basketball?"

That was the last question twelve-year-old Lisa Leslie wanted to hear. She was just beginning the seventh grade in Carson, California, a city near Los Angeles, and she was already six feet, two inches tall. She wasn't very comfortable being so much taller than the other children her age. Nearly every day either a teacher or an older student walked up to her and, before they even said hello or introduced themselves, asked Lisa the same old question.

"Why don't you play basketball?"

Exasperated at being asked the same question over and over, Lisa often answered, "Because I hate it!" She was so tired of the question that she decided she hated basketball and never wanted to play.

Still, that didn't stop anyone from asking her if she

1

played. In desperation, Lisa finally decided to give the game a try. She thought that if she did, people might stop asking her about it.

One day she went to the local playground, Victoria Park, which had some outdoor basketball courts. She asked the boys her age who played there if she could play, too. Since most of the boys were at least six inches shorter than Lisa, they were glad to have someone her height on their side. Despite the fact that she had barely played the game before, she was a good athlete and quickly learned how to rebound and block shots. And if she got the ball close to the basket, she was almost certain to score. None of the boys could jump high enough to block her shots.

To her surprise, she soon discovered that she enjoyed playing. She became friends with the other players at the playground and quickly improved. Now when someone asked her, "Why don't you play basketball?" she held her head up high and said, "I do."

Later that fall, all the boys she played with at the playground joined a local youth basketball league that played at the park. One of the boys on the team asked Lisa if she'd like to join them.

She thought for a moment, then said, "Sure." There wasn't a separate league for girls, so if she wanted to play, she would have to play with the boys. She wanted to play, so she joined the all-boys team.

At the team's first game, Lisa started at center. Every time her team brought the ball up-court, Lisa stood under the basket waving her hands and asking for the ball. But time after time her teammates ignored her. They kept the ball to themselves and tried to make difficult shots.

The coach of Lisa's team called a time-out. Her team was falling far behind.

"Hey!" the coach yelled at his players. "What are you doing? She's wide open under the basket! Give Lisa the ball!"

Lisa's teammates looked at the ground. Even though they knew Lisa was a good player, they were embarrassed to play in front of other boys with a girl on their team. But they were also embarrassed to be so far behind so early in the game. They realized that the coach was right. If they wanted to win, they had to play together as a team.

They went back onto the court, and when the referee blew his whistle, they put the ball into play.

Lisa worked her way under the basket and waved for the ball. One of her teammates lofted a pass in her direction.

Lisa jumped up, caught the ball, and held it high over her head. The boys on the other team tried to jump up and knock it out of her hands, but they were too short and couldn't reach it. Then Lisa spun around, keeping one foot on the ground in one place so she wouldn't be called for traveling. She jumped and shot the ball toward the basket.

It rattled around the rim and then dropped through. Two points!

Lisa's teammates cheered and slapped her on the back as she ran back down-court to play defense. As she remembered later, "They got me the ball and we won."

Ever since that day, Lisa Leslie has gotten the ball every time she has stepped onto a basketball court. More often than not, her team has won. Playing the game she once hated has taken her all around the world, provided a college education, put her picture on the cover of fashion magazines, and given her the opportunity to earn an Olympic gold medal. Today, as a star player for the Los Angeles Sparks of the

Women's National Basketball Association, she earns her living playing basketball. She is considered one of the best female basketball players ever.

Lisa is still approached by strangers who ask her questions. But now they don't ask her, "Do you play basketball?" Instead, they usually ask, "Can I have your autograph?"

The girl who hated basketball has come a long way.

Chapter Two:
1972–1985

Learning to Stand Tall

Lisa Leslie was born on July 7, 1972, the second child of Walter and Christine Leslie. She grew up in Compton, California, a city near Los Angeles.

When Lisa was four years old and her older sister, Dionne, was nine, their parents split up. Walter Leslie left home, never to return. All of a sudden, Christine Leslie was alone, a single mother with two young daughters to take care of.

Christine Leslie was proud and hardworking. She promised herself to do the best she could to take care of her children. She got a job with the post office as a letter carrier. While she worked, Lisa and her sister stayed with a baby-sitter when they weren't in school.

Life wasn't easy for Christine, but she didn't complain. After walking miles each day delivering the mail, she came home and spent time with her children. She took care of the house, made sure that both girls finished their homework, and did her best to see that her daughters were happy and healthy.

Both Dionne and Lisa were tall even when they were very young. When Lisa was in second grade, her teacher, who was five-foot-two, called her mother and said, "I was wondering if you knew your daughter is taller than everyone in the class, including me."

Christine Leslie just laughed. Everyone in Lisa's family was tall. Walter Leslie was six-foot-five, and Christine was six-foot-three. Both parents had played basketball in high school. Walter Leslie had been so good that when he was a young man, he had even earned extra money playing for a local semiprofessional team.

Christine knew what it was like to be the tallest girl in her class. While she was growing up, she had often been teased. It had been a painful experience, and for a long time she had been embarrassed by her height.

She wanted to make sure that neither of her daughters ever felt the same way. She stood tall and took great pride in her appearance. Every chance she had, she told the girls that they were beautiful and intelligent and that if they worked hard, they could accomplish anything they wanted to. She told them that being so tall was a sign that they were descended from African royalty and that they should feel honored. Her favorite saying was "Being tall is nothing to be ashamed of."

When she bought the girls new school clothes at the end of each summer, she held a pretend fashion show so they'd feel good about themselves. She taught them how to walk like fashion models and turn around to show off their clothes. Then the girls would dress in their favorite outfits and model for their mother and her friends and relatives.

Dionne and Lisa loved the fashion shows so much that Christine eventually sent the girls to a local charm school, where they were taught by a woman who had once worked with professional models. They had to practice walking with books balanced on their heads and were taught proper manners and how to dress. Once in a while, they even got to model for real at shows put on by the charm school and local merchants. Lisa and her sister both grew up to be confident and proud.

But that didn't mean they were never teased. At school, some kids still called Lisa "Olive Oyl," after the tall, skinny character in the *Popeye* cartoons. Although the jeers bothered Lisa, she tried not to let it show. Her mother told her to ignore the taunts. "Someone is always going to say something negative," she said. "But small minds, you don't pay attention to." Besides, she teased, someday those boys calling you names will be calling for a date!

When Lisa was nine years old, her mother decided to quit her job at the post office. By this time, she had another daughter, Tiffany, who was only two. It was hard to raise her children on a letter carrier's salary.

Christine learned how to drive a big eighteen-wheel tractor-trailer and became a long-distance truck driver, called a long-hauler. At the beginning of each trip, she loaded her truck with goods that needed to be hauled to the East Coast, then spent four or five days driving across country, sleeping at truck stops in a small bunk in the back of her truck's cab. After she delivered the goods, she picked up another load and returned with it to California.

Although there were very few women working as long-haulers, nothing stopped Christine Leslie. She was confident of her own abilities and knew she could drive a truck as well as any man could.

She made a lot more money, but her job took her away from home for days at a time. Her children were too young to stay at home by themselves, so Christine had to hire a live-in housekeeper to watch over them.

Lisa was proud of her mother, but she was sad each time she went away. To make herself feel better, Lisa would spend hours looking through the family photo album, gazing at pictures that showed her together with her mother and her sisters.

"There were some sad times," she once told a reporter. "Mom had to travel so far away. But we understood. It made me mature really fast."

With their mother gone so much, Lisa and her sisters realized that they had to help one another out and be responsible. Each girl did chores such as cleaning the house and doing laundry. They knew that every time their mother returned home, she was exhausted from driving. They wanted her to be proud of them.

When school let out for summer vacation, there was no need for a live-in housekeeper. Lisa's mother wanted the family to spend as much time together as possible, so they'd all pile into the big cab of her truck and spend the summer driving back and forth across the country.

It was sometimes tough traveling so much, but overall the family enjoyed it. Lisa and her sisters got to see the entire country, from the Rocky Mountains to the wheat fields of the Midwest, to big cities such as New York and Chicago. They read books to one another, sang songs, laughed, and sometimes argued. But they were together, and that was all that mattered.

Although they occasionally slept in motels, they usually shared the small bunk in the back of the cab. "We had to hold on to one another," Lisa once told a reporter, laughing. "That probably helped us. We hold on to one another now in a lot of ways."

But as the girls grew older — and bigger — Lisa's mother realized that they couldn't spend the entire summer with her. Dionne and Lisa were teenagers and becoming involved in all sorts of activities. It would be hard for them to make friends and do things with other kids if they spent each summer playing truck driver.

So when Lisa entered junior high, her mother had the three girls move in with her sister in Carson, California, near Los Angeles. That was much better than staying with a housekeeper. Lisa's aunt had several children of her own, and Lisa enjoyed having cousins to play with.

When Lisa was in eighth grade at Whaley Junior High, a classmate whom she admired approached her. Usually, the girl ignored Lisa.

The girl had heard from some of the other students that Lisa had played basketball on a boys team. There was an eighth grade girls basketball team, and the girl was planning to try out. She asked Lisa if she'd like to try out as well.

Lisa had enjoyed playing at Victoria Park and with the boys team, but she hadn't really thought about playing in junior high. Still, she wanted to make friends, and basketball seemed like a good way to do it. She agreed to give it a try.

The next day at tryouts, Lisa couldn't believe how good some of the girls were. It was obvious that they had been playing basketball for years. Many dribbled the ball and shot just as well as the boys did.

Lisa, on the other hand, had always relied on her height to help her play well. Now she realized that she didn't share the skills the other girls had. She didn't even know how to shoot a layup.

But when you are thirteen years old and more than six feet tall, basketball coaches notice you. The first thing the coach did was show Lisa how to shoot a layup. As she made her first attempt, Lisa later remembered thinking, If I fall down, I'm quitting and never playing this game again.

Guess what?

Lisa didn't fall down. She kept playing basketball.

Chapter Three:
1985–1988

Reaching for Goals

All of a sudden, basketball became a big part of Lisa's life. The girls team went undefeated, winning all seven of its games. Lisa got to play a lot and had fun. She made some new friends, and her game began to improve.

But with the school's short basketball season over, she was without a team. Then one day she mentioned her love of the sport to her cousin Craig Simpson.

Craig played basketball for Dorsey High School. He spent almost every waking moment at the local gym, working out or playing basketball with his friends.

Craig knew that a girl as tall as Lisa had a chance to be a very good player if she worked hard enough. Few woman are more than six feet tall, so her height would be a tremendous advantage on the court. He saw Lisa's potential and decided to make certain she made the most of it. Besides, he figured he'd enjoy having someone in the family to play basketball with.

"That was it," Lisa later remembered. "Working with my cousin is how I got my skills. He made me do all kinds of things."

As soon as Lisa finished school, she went home and did her homework. Then Craig took her to the gym. He told her that if she was willing to work hard, he thought she could become a very good player.

But Craig knew that simply playing basketball wouldn't be enough to ensure that Lisa reached her full potential. First she had to get in shape.

Before he allowed Lisa to touch a basketball, he put her through a rigorous workout of sit-ups, push-ups, and other exercises, such as jumping rope. After only a few days, Lisa, sore and tired, complained, "I'm not going to do this anymore." She wanted to play basketball, not exercise.

Craig just looked at her. "Lisa, I'll tell you what," he said. "You can either do it, or this is the end of your basketball career. I won't take you to the gym anymore."

Lisa reluctantly agreed to keep exercising. Deep down, she knew he was right. Craig was trying to help her increase her stamina and become strong. It was nice to be tall, but there more to being a basketball player than height.

Then Craig began teaching Lisa the fundamentals of the game. He had her practice dribbling with each hand and taught her the various kinds of passes used in basketball, such as the chest pass, bounce pass, and baseball pass. He worked on her shooting, too, teaching her the jump shot and hook shot.

As Lisa improved, she and Craig played games one-on-one so she could work on her defense and practice her new skills in a competitive situation. Even though Lisa was taller, Craig always won. He was still a much better player. Yet day by day, Lisa slowly began to improve.

When Craig felt Lisa was ready, he invited her to play in pickup games with his friends at the gym. He felt that if she played against boys, particularly boys who were better players and more experienced, her game would improve more rapidly than if she played with just girls.

Lisa had never worked so hard in her life. After each session at the gym, she went home and collapsed from fatigue. But at the same time, she took great pride in her progress. She could feel her body getting stronger. Her coordination improved dramatically. She could tell that she was getting better.

At first, the boys she played with rarely passed her the ball. Like her old boys team, they ignored her. They didn't think she had the skills yet to put the ball on the floor or shoot. It was frustrating for Lisa. But instead of getting discouraged, she concentrated on playing defense and rebounding, two aspects of the game that are often overlooked in pickup games.

Because she was willing to do this "dirty work," the boys soon began to respect her. It wasn't long before they forgot that she was a girl and started passing her the ball.

Lisa worked out with Craig nearly every day for a whole year. At the end of the summer, the family moved to Inglewood, another city just outside Los

Angeles. When school started, she enrolled in Morningside High School.

The school had a strong athletic program. In most sports, the Morningside Monarchs were one of the best teams in the Los Angeles area.

That included the girls basketball team. Coach Frank Scott's Lady Monarchs were a powerhouse, perennial champions of the Ocean League.

When Lisa went to tryouts, she was nervous. She was only a freshman and didn't know many of the other players, most of whom had already played together. She knew the team was good and wasn't certain whether she would be good enough to make the squad.

Coach Scott noticed Lisa right away. But he didn't expect much. He knew that many tall teenagers aren't well coordinated, particularly those who are only fourteen.

Lisa was different. After having worked out with Craig, she moved well. Coach Scott quickly realized that she knew what she was doing on the basketball court.

Lisa was surprised, too. She hadn't played basketball against other girls in nearly a year. But all the hard work she had done with her cousin Craig was paying off. Although Lisa wasn't a standout, she could hold her own against older, more experienced players.

She made the starting lineup and played center, a position that took advantage of her height. Morningside had a good season, and by the end of the year, Lisa had become one of the best players on the team. When she got the ball close to the basket, she was almost unstoppable. Playing against boys had made her an aggressive, physical player. Basketball coaches all around southern California began to hear about the emerging star from Morningside.

The next year continued her upward trend. While senior forward Shaundra Greene, a high school all-American and one of the best players in the country, was the team's standout, Lisa began to give the competition fits. She reached her full height of six-foot-five and just kept playing better. Most other teams couldn't keep up with Morningside. On defense, the Monarchs utilized a full-court press. On offense, they played aggressive, fast-break basketball.

Lisa's primary responsibility on the team was to get rebounds and play defense. Whenever opponents penetrated to the basket, they had to worry about Lisa jumping out and blocking their shot. And even if they got the ball over Lisa's hands, she often forced them to change their shot. If it missed, she snagged the rebound and quickly passed it down the court to start the fast break.

It didn't get easier for the opposition once the Lady Monarchs got the ball. Unless she was double-teamed, Shaundra Greene could score almost at will, either by driving strongly toward the hoop for a layup or by pulling up and sinking a jump shot. And even when Greene was covered, Lisa or another player was usually open. Most of Lisa's points came on wide-open layups or after she snagged an offensive rebound and put the ball back into the basket. For the season, Lisa averaged 21.3 points, 12.2 rebounds, and 6.1 blocked shots per game.

The team raced through the regular season, going undefeated in their league and losing only one game outside their league. They easily qualified for the state tournament.

They continued to be successful in the tournament, running their record to 33–1. They won the California Southern Section 4-A title and qualified for the state championship.

They met Northern Section champion Fremont in the Oakland Coliseum on March 19, 1988. Thousands of people filled the stands to watch the two best girls basketball teams in the state of California battle it out.

Morningside started out fast. Their pressure defense forced Fremont into making mistakes that the Monarchs converted into baskets. And even when Fremont broke the press, it hardly mattered, because Lisa Leslie was standing strong in the middle.

The Fremont offense centered around two high-scoring stars, Debra Davis and Sonjhia Fleming, who were among the best inside players in the state. But Lisa wasn't intimidated. Each time Davis or Fleming tried to go inside, she jumped up and swatted at the ball. In the first half, she blocked an amazing seven shots, three of which led directly to fast-break scores by Morningside. Davis and Fleming scored only a combined sixteen points, and Morningside led at the half, 34–24.

But Fremont didn't give up. In the third quarter, Morningside started to run out of steam while Fremont patiently chipped away at its lead. Entering the fourth quarter, Morningside led by only six points, 41–35.

Then, in the first four minutes of the fourth quarter, Morningside appeared to get its second wind. The Lady Monarchs pushed the ball up-court and stretched their lead to eight points with only four minutes remaining in the game.

The Monarchs should have kept attacking. Instead, they tried to slow down the game and preserve their lead. But that wasn't the way they played best.

That's all the help Fremont needed. All of a sudden, they were the aggressors and the Monarchs were back on their heels. Fremont scored nine unanswered points to go ahead, 53–52.

The Monarchs had the ball. They passed it around the perimeter, and then, with only a second or two remaining, snapped it to Lisa, along the baseline.

She knew time was running out. As quickly as she could, she spun and shot a short jumper from six feet.

The ball hit the rim and bounced up. Then it hit the rim again and bounced out.

BZZZZ! The game was over. Morningside lost, 53–52. The Monarchs hadn't scored a single point in the last four minutes of the game. While the Fremont players jumped up and down in celebration, the Morningside girls tried to hold back sobs.

Lisa and her teammates were crushed. They knew they should have won. "We slowed it down a little," admitted guard JoJo Witherspoon. Added Shaundra Greene, "We made simple mistakes, and we let it slow down."

Lisa was in tears. All she could say was "This game snuck up on us."

On the long trip back to Inglewood, Lisa had time to think. She was only a sophomore. She promised herself that if she made it into a championship game again, she wouldn't miss out on the opportunity to win. She only had one goal — to win the state championship.

Only a few weeks later, however, Lisa added a second goal to her wish list. The United States national women's team came to California and played an exhibition game. Lisa and some of her teammates went to watch.

She was mesmerized. When she saw the team on court in their colorful red-white-and-blue uniforms with *USA* emblazoned across the fronts, she knew exactly what she wanted to do.

"It was at that moment," she remembered later, "that I made it my goal to play in the Olympics and win the gold medal."

But first she had to finish high school.

Chapter Four:
1988-1989

Slamming Star

In the summer and fall before her junior year of high school, Lisa worked out longer and harder than she ever had before. With the graduation of Shaundra Greene, she knew she was destined to become a bigger part of Morningside's offense, and she wanted to be ready. She was also increasingly aware of all the things that basketball could do for her — if she was prepared.

During her sophomore year, Lisa had occasionally received letters from college coaches who were interested in having her play basketball for their school. Due to a government regulation known as Title IX, colleges had to treat men's and women's athletic programs equally and offer the same number of scholarships to women as they did to men. Star players such as Lisa were recruited as intensely as the best male players.

By the beginning of her junior year, Lisa's mailbox was full almost every day and the phone rang almost nonstop as coaches from around the country tried to convince her to attend their school. Dozens of colleges were prepared to offer her a full four-year scholarship as soon as she graduated from high school.

She knew how important that was. A scholarship to college would save her family thousands of dollars. Lisa was determined to make the most of her opportunity.

Her mother helped keep her on track. She made sure her daughter realized that schoolwork came first. Unless she had good grades and test scores, the scholarships would not come through. Lisa carried a 3.5 grade average and took honors courses whenever she could.

Her mother also encouraged her to get involved in other school activities. She was elected president of her class in her sophomore, junior, and senior years. She was also a member of the girls volleyball team and competed in sprints, the high jump, and long jump on the track team.

But basketball remained number one on Lisa's list. She hadn't forgotten her promise to herself to win the state championship.

Despite the loss of Shaundra Greene, the Monarchs were loaded. JoJo Witherspoon was one of the most sought-after guards in the country, and everyone expected Lisa to be even better than she had been the year before. Before the season even started, Morningside was ranked the number one team in California and one of the ten best high school basketball teams in the country.

Lisa was determined to help Morningside keep its high rank. During practice before the start of the season, she began doing something that virtually no other female high school basketball player could do. She started dunking the basketball!

Although other girls as tall as Lisa, and even taller, had played high school basketball, none were as athletic as she was. And while a few had probably been able to dunk if they had a running start, no one could dunk as easily as Lisa could. She needed only to take a step or two to be able to jump above the rim. Even many male basketball players of Lisa's height couldn't dunk the ball.

She loved how it felt to jump up high with the ball in her hands and jam it down through the hoop. Her teammates loved it, too. When the season started, they were determined to help her dunk during a game, something no girl had ever done in a high school game.

She didn't waste any time. In Morningside's season opener, against Manual Arts, the Monarchs got the ball and started their fast break. Lisa raced down the court ahead of everyone else. A teammate hit her on the run with a prefect pass.

Without breaking stride, Lisa caught the pass and jumped, soaring toward the hoop as she lifted the ball above her head. At the apex of her leap, she jammed the ball through the net.

Everyone in the bleachers roared approval. Lisa's teammates quickly surrounded her and gave her a quick hug or pat on the back before the game resumed. Morningside went on to win easily.

After the game, Lisa was surprised to learn that not only was she the first girl to slam-dunk in a high school game but she was also only the second American woman of any age to do so in a game. For a while, everyone called her "Dunkin'." The rest of her high school career, she usually dunked the ball at least once during a game.

Lisa was quickly becoming famous. Her opponents already knew all about her. They dreaded playing Morningside, because it was almost impossible to keep her from scoring.

In one contest in the middle of the season, against Redondo, Lisa was matched up against Vanessa Vogelsang, a six-foot two-inch center who averaged more than twenty-five points per game. Vogelsang was considered to be one of the best players in the state. But Lisa wasn't intimidated. Instead, she became the intimidator.

In the opening minutes of the game, Lisa made Vogelsang's head spin by sinking three straight baskets. On defense, she was just as dominating. Vogelsang couldn't even get a shot off. Every time she tried, Lisa swatted the ball away.

Redondo coach Tim Ammentorp quickly called a time-out to settle his team down. Vogelsang had had enough. She told her coach, "I can't play against her." He became upset and removed her from the game. Morningside romped to a 77–11 win.

After the game, Lisa was philosophical. She didn't like to embarrass an opponent, but as she told a reporter, "I can tell when people are intimidated. When I see a weakness, that's when I feel it's time for me to take over because they're scared of me."

Ammentorp agreed. "Leslie intimidated everyone in the gym," he said after the game. "We had people who didn't want to bring the ball up-court. We had people open, but we wouldn't throw it because Lisa was there."

Morningside stormed through the regular season, destroying the opposition with ease. Their only loss came in a tournament against Southern High of Louisville, Kentucky, 52–50. Even then, Lisa was named tournament MVP.

Lisa was more than just a great high school player. She was becoming a great player, period. Coach Scott called her "unstoppable," and a collegiate scout pegged her "the number one underclassman in the country." As a junior, she was already one of the best two or three high school players to ever come from southern California.

The Monarchs easily qualified for the state tournament. They entered the semifinals for the Southern District championship against San Diego/Point Loma without even being tested by the opposition.

In the first five minutes of the game, the Monarchs were clicking on all cylinders. They led 17–0. There didn't seem to be any question about whether Morningside would win the game. The only question was by how much.

But then Lisa got into foul trouble and had to play carefully. She didn't want to take a chance on fouling out.

That gave Point Loma the opportunity to get back in the game. By halftime, Morningside led by only three points, 30–27, as Lisa was forced to the bench with four fouls. If she committed one more, she would foul out of the game.

In the second half, Lisa sat out most of the third quarter. Both teams played carefully, and Point Loma even went ahead, 36–30, before Lisa reentered the game and led Morningside on a comeback.

Yet with only a minute left to play, Point Loma pulled ahead again. They led, 44–43.

Then Lisa got the ball. With only a minute

remaining in the game, there was no reason to be cautious.

She got the ball close to the basket and went for the hoop, scoring on an eight-foot turn-around jumper. Morningside led, 45–44.

With only twenty-seven seconds left to play, Point Loma turned the ball over. Morningside tried to run out the clock, but JoJo Witherspoon was fouled. She missed the front end of a one-and-one. Lisa got the rebound, but her put-back missed, too.

Point Loma had the ball, needing only a basket to win.

But in the excitement of the game, a Point Loma player lost track of the time. Although seven seconds remained in the game, the girl threw up a desperation shot from thirty feet.

It rattled off the backboard and into JoJo Witherspoon's hands. Morningside won, 45–44. Lisa's final basket had won the game.

The victory set up a rematch with Fremont for the state championship. This time, Lisa was determined not to let the game hinge on a last-second shot.

But when the two teams met on the court, it was

obvious that Fremont was confident. They had beaten Morningside the previous year and weren't intimidated by Lisa. In the first quarter, they jumped ahead.

Then Lisa took over. She scored nineteen first-half points to give Morningside a thirteen-point lead at the break.

At halftime, the girls reminded each other what had happened during the game with Fremont the previous year. They were determined not to squander their lead.

In the second half, Lisa focused on defense and shut down Fremont. Her teammates got the fast break going. Morningside won, 60–50, and Lisa finished with 21 points, 14 rebounds, and 4 blocked shots. This time, when the final buzzer sounded, it was Morningside that did the celebrating while Fremont left the court in tears.

"We felt really hurt after last year," Lisa said after the game. "We knew we had the better team and we still lost. That hurt."

Now things were different. "It didn't matter to us how much we won by," she added. "We just wanted to win." Already, the press was writing about Morningside's chance to repeat as champions during the 1989–1990 season.

But basketball season wasn't over for Lisa. She had been invited to try out for the United States national team scheduled to play in the Olympic Festival later that summer. The national team, made up primarily of high school players, was part of a "feeder system" designed to support the United States women's Olympic team. The best players would probably advance to the United States junior team, for players under the age of twenty-one. This team, usually consisting of college players, competed for the Junior World Championship. Only the very best from that team would be invited to try out for the national team and play in the Olympics.

But a funny thing happened on Lisa's way to the Olympic Festival. She was already so good, she was invited to try out for the junior team. She skipped the high school Olympic Festival team entirely.

Despite the fact that she had to try out against college players who were as much as three years older than she was and far more experienced, Lisa easily made the team. In fact, she made the starting lineup.

In July 1989, Lisa traveled with the team to Bilbao, Spain, for the Junior World Championship. The competition included teams from basketball powerhouse countries such as the Soviet Union, Yugoslavia, and Australia.

American squads are often at a disadvantage in such tournaments. International basketball rules are slightly different, favoring less aggressive play, and American players have to make adjustments. Also, national teams from many other countries have the opportunity to train and practice together all year long. American teams, except for the Olympic squad, usually have only a few months to prepare.

The Americans dropped their first two games, losing to South Korea in overtime and to Australia by two points. But they played well. Lisa had been strong, scoring seventeen points and pulling down nine rebounds in the heartbreak game against Australia.

The team collected its first win in game three, against Bulgaria, 78–65. Lisa paced the U.S. attack with twenty-two points. Then, playing their fourth game in four days, the Americans lost to powerful Czechoslovakia, 90–87. Lisa collected sixteen rebounds.

The team bounced back to win two of its last three games, finishing the tournament in seventh place with a respectable 3–4 record. But the big news for the United States was the play of Lisa Leslie.

She hadn't just played well; she had played great. In the seven-game tournament, she led the U.S. team with an average of 13.3 points, 7 rebounds, and 3 blocked shots per game. She scored the most field goals, the most free throws, and even picked up eight steals. All this while she was the youngest player on the team and one of the youngest players in the entire tournament!

When word about Lisa's performance got around, every high school girls basketball team let loose a big groan. Because Lisa Leslie still had one year left to play in high school. She was only going to get better.

Chapter Five:
1989-1990

The Numbers Game

When Lisa took the court during her senior year, she did so as the consensus pick for best girls high school basketball player in the country. As they had been the previous year, the Morningside Lady Monarchs were ranked as the number one girls basketball team in California and as one of the ten best girls basketball teams in the country. Lisa Leslie was the reason.

Other girls might have felt pressure, but Lisa was different. She thrived under the expectation to be the best, both on the court and off. In late December of 1989, she was even selected as the female winner of the Dial Award, a prestigious honor given to the top scholar-athlete in the nation.

Morningside was strong from the start. Although the Monarchs stumbled and lost several games in big tournaments that included teams from all over the country, they still stormed through the Ocean League without a defeat. Lisa was playing better than ever.

They entered the last week of league play with the championship clinched and a record of 20–3. Only two home games, against South Torrance and Centennial, remained to be played.

Lisa was looking forward to the South Torrance game. She'd been thinking about it for weeks.

Because the Monarchs were so good, Coach Scott usually kept the team in check. He didn't allow them to run up the score against their opponents, although sometimes they still won by fifty or sixty points. That meant that Lisa was often removed from the lineup early in the game. Even though she rarely played much more than half of every game, she was still averaging nearly thirty points per contest.

Other coaches appreciated Scott's gesture. For as one had said of Lisa the previous season, "If she was on my team, she'd score fifty points a game."

The girls didn't mind being held in check, however, because for one game every year, the league finale, Coach Scott didn't try to keep the score down. On defense, he kept his team in a full-court press the entire game, no matter what the score was. And on offense, he selected one senior and in his words, "let her loose," to try to score as many points as she possibly could. He instructed the Monarchs that whenever they got the ball, they should pass it to that senior player.

In another year, Scott would have chosen the Centennial game, their regular season finale, to spotlight a senior. But earlier in the year, a fight had broken out between Morningside and Centennial during a game. He was afraid that if he cut his team loose against Centennial, it might turn ugly. So South Torrance received the dubious honor instead.

Scott reasoned that his players had worked hard and followed his instructions all year long, so in one game, they deserved to have some fun. Two years before, in the league finale against El Segundo, Shaundra Greene had scored sixty-one points. The previous season, against South Torrance, JoJo Witherspoon had scored sixty-eight. This time Scott selected Lisa as the designated senior.

Even before the game had started, Morningside

fans were wondering how many points Lisa might be able to score. Some even thought she had a chance to break the national high school girls record of 106 points set by Riverside Poly's Cheryl Miller in 1982. Miller, the older sister of Indiana Pacer star Reggie Miller, had gone on to play in the Olympics and was considered the best female basketball player of all time.

But it's hard to score one hundred points in any game, particularly a high school game. In high school, each quarter is only eight minutes long, so to score one hundred points, a player has to score more than three points a minute. Most basketball players would have a hard time scoring that many points in an empty gym if they had to run up and down the court after each time they made a basket.

Even before the game started, South Torrance was at a tremendous disadvantage. They were in a rebuilding year to begin with and had been further decimated by injuries. They only had six girls in uniform that were available to play.

Before the tip-off, Lisa and her teammates told the opposition what to expect. They wanted South Torrance to understand why they were going to play the way they were. It was only fair, and besides, by giving South Torrance plenty of warning, they were letting them know that the ball was going to be passed to Lisa every time Morningside got the ball. They could have all five players cover Lisa if they wanted to.

As soon as the ball was put into play, the Monarchs went into action. Lisa controlled the tip and raced toward the Morningside basket. A teammate fired a pass into her hands, and she laid it in the basket. Only a few seconds had ticked off the clock.

When South Torrance tried to put the ball in play, the Morningside players swarmed over them. They stole a pass, and Lisa scored again. That's the way it was all game long.

South Torrance tried as hard as they could to stop Lisa. Before the game was a minute old, they had resorted to having all five players try to cover Lisa, keeping two people behind her while the other three tried to keep her from getting her hands on the ball.

But Lisa couldn't be stopped. She towered over her opponents. Her teammates lofted passes in her direction, and Lisa simply jumped up and caught them. Once she had the ball, the only way South Torrance could stop her was by fouling her. Yet even when South Torrance got rough, throwing elbows at Lisa and bloodying her lip, they were powerless to keep her from scoring.

When the buzzer sounded to end the first quarter, Lisa looked up at the scoreboard. As she recalled later, "I looked up and it showed us up, 49–6. I asked, 'Is this the half?'"

She was already so tired, she started to walk off the court before being pulled back by her team-mates.

It wasn't the half after all. In just one quarter, Lisa had scored forty-nine points! No other Morningside player had scored a point, while South Torrance was still in single digits.

When Lisa realized she had scored nearly fifty points and that there were still three quarters to go, it dawned on her that she had a good chance to break Cheryl Miller's record.

The second quarter was a carbon copy of the first, only now Morningside let South Torrance score a few easy baskets so they could get the ball back more quickly. The South Torrance players were so frustrated by how the game was going that they were fouling Lisa almost every time she got the ball. But that didn't stop her. She was a good free-throw shooter, and as far as she was concerned, it didn't matter whether she scored from the field or the free-throw line.

In the final moments of the first half, two South Torrance players fouled out. One of Lisa's teammates, Sherrell Young, made a foul shot to become the only Morningside player other than Lisa to score. When the halftime buzzer sounded, Lisa looked at the scoreboard.

It read *Morningside 102, Visitors 24.* In only sixteen minutes of play, Lisa had scored 101 points!

After a brief break, Morningside ran back out onto the court to begin the second half. Lisa needed only five more points to break Cheryl Miller's record!

But South Torrance coach Gil Ramirez had only four girls still eligible to play. Fed up, he refused to send his team back out onto the court to start the second half.

Though she appreciated how he felt, Lisa couldn't let her chance just slip by. She asked Coach Ramirez if he would send his team out onto the court long enough for her to score the necessary points and break the record. Ramirez asked his team, but they said no. Like their coach, they had had enough.

Coach Scott still sent Morningside back onto the floor. When the officials blew the whistle to start the second half and South Torrance didn't come out onto the floor, they whistled again and called a technical foul for delay of the game. Lisa made the foul shot, then made three more to tie the record as the official kept calling technical fouls.

Then they stopped the game. There was no sense even trying to continue.

After the game, the officials decided that they had been incorrect to call all but the first technical foul, so Lisa really didn't tie the record after all. Officially, she finished with 102 points. Morningside won, 103–24.

In an amazing performance, Lisa had taken 56 shots from the field, making 37, and made 28 of 36 free throws. In sixteen minutes of play, she averaged six points a minute, or a point every ten seconds!

Still, Coach Scott's decision to let Lisa run with the ball was heavily criticized after the game. In reply, Coach Scott told the press that "Lisa could have broken the record in her sophomore year" if he had let her. "And she could have averaged fifty points a game," he added.

Lisa was happy but exhausted after the game. When asked if she felt sorry for South Torrance, she said, "It wasn't personal. They knew I was going for the record." As if to emphasize the point, she also noted that she didn't even try to dunk once during the entire game. If she had, she might have legitimately set the record. Most of her points had come on short jumpers.

Then she added, "It's hard to believe I did it. I'm kind of disappointed that I didn't break the record, but it's kind of obvious I would have."

That was the understatement of the year.

The next day, after word of her accomplishment had spread across the country, Lisa was mobbed by the press in front of her home. Newspapers all around the country carried stories about the game, and Lisa was even the subject of a story in *Sports Illustrated* magazine.

She enjoyed the attention. But as she was soon to discover, there was a price to be paid for her new-found fame.

Chapter Six:
1990

Senior Star

For the third consecutive season, the Morningside Monarchs entered the state tournament as odds-on favorites to repeat as state champions. But they knew they still had to play well in order to win.

Morningside had a surprisingly difficult time. As the Monarchs' leader on both offense and defense, Lisa felt that it was her responsibility to make sure the team played aggressively.

But Lisa wasn't just another player on the team. As the best player in girls high school basketball, she was the focal point of every game she played in. Morningside's opponents knew that in order to win, they had to do something about Lisa.

They played her hard and tough and tried to use her own aggressiveness against her. The referees unintentionally cooperated. Under the increased scrutiny that often takes place during tournament time, Lisa's aggressive play led her to be called for more than her usual share of fouls by the officials. In several games, she was saddled with foul trouble.

Fortunately, Morningside wasn't a one-woman team. With Lisa on the bench for extended periods, her teammates picked up the slack, and Morningside still managed to win the Southern Division to qualify for the championship game. Their opponent would be the Berkeley Yellow Jackets, the Northern Division champions.

The two teams weren't strangers to each other. During Lisa's junior year, Morningside had defeated Berkeley. Lisa hadn't played particularly well that game, though, and she looked forward to playing better in the rematch.

Only two days before the championship game, Berkeley Coach Gene Nakamura inadvertently gave Lisa some added motivation. He told a reporter that his team wasn't "awed" by Morningside and boasted that in their meeting the previous season, Berkeley center Jualeah Woods had "outplayed" Lisa. He was so confident of victory that he announced that his team planned to play Lisa "head up" — meaning that they didn't plan to try any double-teams or other special defense.

In practice the day before the game, Coach Scott read the entire article to his team. Everyone, particularly Lisa, got fired up. She didn't think any team in the state could play her "head up."

The two teams meet in Oakland on March 17, 1990, to play for the state championship. Hundreds of Morningside fans made the long trip up the California coast to watch. The Oakland Coliseum was packed to capacity.

Waiting in the locker room before the game, Lisa was uncharacteristically quiet. Usually she moved around the room from player to player, cracking jokes or trying to fire her team up. Today, she seemed withdrawn.

At first, Coach Scott and her teammates thought Lisa was just trying to focus on the game. But Lisa finally approached Coach Scott and told him she didn't feel well.

In fact, she felt awful. She was feverish and a little nauseous. She knew her own body well enough to know that it was more than just a case of nerves.

A few weeks before, her little sister, Tiffany, had come down with the chicken pox. Most children get the disease when they are very young and become immune to further attacks. But somehow, Lisa had either avoided the malady or had contracted a very weak case that left her open to another infection. Although she had yet to develop the itchy sores that characterize the illness, she was almost certain she was getting the chicken pox. What a time to get sick!

Yet Lisa insisted on playing, and Coach Scott agreed. However, he warned Lisa that if she became too sick to play, he would remove her from the game.

After the jump ball that opened the game, both teams played cautiously, probing each other, looking for a weak spot. Late in the first quarter, Berkeley went ahead, 12–9.

Lisa had a hard time getting started. She found it difficult to ignore her symptoms and concentrate. Besides, she didn't want to get into foul trouble. But when she looked up at the scoreboard and saw that her team was behind, she forgot about being sick. She started playing her game.

Lisa sparked a run. She made a couple of strong moves to the basket, and it became clear that no one on the Berkeley team was really capable of playing her "head up." With Lisa suddenly drawing the attention of the Berkeley defense, Morningside's sophomore forward, Janet Davis, was left wide open.

Morningside ran off fifteen unanswered points as Davis scored six points during the run and Lisa added five. Early in the second quarter, Morningside led, 23–12.

Desperate to stop Lisa and almost powerless to do so, Berkeley center Jualeah Woods picked up her third foul. Coach Nakamura had little choice but to bench her and hope Berkeley stayed close until it was late enough in the game for her to return.

Keyed by point guard Tanda Rucker, who scored twenty-five points for the game, Berkeley fought back. With less than five minutes left to play in the game, the Yellow Jackets trailed Morningside by only three points, 52–49.

Although she felt ill, Lisa was playing great and had already scored twenty-two points. But now was the time to play even better.

On four consecutive trips down the floor, Morningside got the ball to Lisa on the inside. She was a whirlwind, soaring to the basket for layups and spinning to shoot her jumper. She scored four straight baskets, and suddenly Morningside's lead was back in double figures.

Berkeley never recovered. As Lisa scored 13 of the Monarchs' last 15 points, Morningside rolled to a convincing 67–56 victory. Lisa finished with a game-high 35 points while hauling down 12 rebounds and blocking 7 shots.

But while her teammates celebrated the win on court, Lisa cut her own revelry short. She was still feeling sick. As a precautionary measure, she went right from the Coliseum to a local hospital, where she was given fluids and diagnosed with the early stages of chicken pox.

Her gutsy performance earned everyone's respect. When a reporter asked Coach Scott if he had been worried when Berkeley closed the gap in the fourth quarter, he replied, "We still had Lisa in the game. Anytime we have her in the game, I feel confident." Then he added, "She wasn't quite as aggressive as usual because she wasn't feeling well. Maybe that was a blessing in disguise." Lisa had stayed out of foul trouble.

Even Coach Nakamura had to admit that he had been wrong about Lisa. "Not many people can guard that six-foot-five girl," he said. "I think she's matured. I've seen her get too emotional and get into foul trouble. She did a great job staying under control tonight."

While Lisa recovered from the chicken pox, the press began to speculate about where she would play basketball in college. Every team in the country wanted her. By April, she had narrowed the candidates to Notre Dame, Long Beach State, and the University of Southern California.

Some observers were surprised by Lisa's interest in USC. After winning the NCAA championship in both 1983 and 1984, the USC women's basketball program had fallen on hard times. The previous season, they had finished with a record of only 8–19.

But USC had hired a new coach, Marianne Stanley. In her last coaching job, at Old Dominion in Virginia, Stanley had won three NCAA titles. She was expected to put USC back on track. In fact, she had already recruited several promising prospects.

Lisa had, in fact, decided to attend USC. But as the press soon found out, there was a problem. Lisa, an honor student and the Dial Award winner, hadn't qualified academically.

According to the rules of the National Collegiate Athletic Association, the governing body that controls collegiate athletics, entering freshman athletes have to score at least 700 out of a possible 1600 on a standardized exam called the Scholastic Aptitude Test, or SAT. While players can still be given scholarships if they fail to score 700, they can't play as freshmen.

Lisa hadn't expected to have any difficulty scoring 700. After all, her grades were good and she took honors courses.

But when she first took the test the previous year, she scored only 680. She thought her performance was a fluke and took it again. She was stunned to learn she again scored only 680.

The SAT is a controversial measure of academic aptitude. Critics argue that the test assumes that all high school programs are the same, when in reality, they vary widely from school district to school district. Others charge that the tests are culturally biased against African-Americans.

Lisa was a good student. She had studied hard at Morningside and done far more work than was required. Yet she had still failed to score high enough on the test.

Lisa admitted that she was embarrassed when word about her test scores got out. But she didn't get discouraged.

The test made her realize that because Morningside was a relatively poor urban school, her education hadn't been as good as it could have been. "The test is basically biased, as far as I'm concerned," she said.

"We should all learn the same things. It shouldn't differ as to what area you live in. A lot of what's on the SAT, we haven't covered in our everyday learning. It might be because of our books. We have the same books the school was using years ago. It's kind of unfair, because we're not all provided with the same materials."

But despite her feelings, she knew she would still

Otto Greule Jr.

University of Southern California superstar Lisa Leslie jogs into position in a game versus Stanford.

Lisa Leslie cries during the gold medal ceremony of the 1996 Olympics.

The calm before the storm: Lisa Leslie's team photo, taken days before the first game of the WNBA's inaugural season.

Los Angeles Sparks center Lisa Leslie skies above the competition in a game versus the Houston Comets.

Lisa battles New York Liberty's Rebecca Lobo for position.

Caught in the middle, Lisa looks for a teammate to save the ball from falling into the hands of the Cleveland Rockers.

A tough woman to push around, Lisa stands her ground against the Phoenix Mercury's Toni Foster.

No pain, no gain: Lisa fights off Houston Coment Tina Thompson.

Lisa drives the baseline, edging past Janice Braxton of the Cleveland Rockers.

Rivals in the WNBA, in the 1997 off-season, Lisa Leslie and Tina Thompson team up with other players for exhibition games in Italy and elsewhere in Europe.

Lisa Leslie's Career Statistics

COLLEGE

Year	Points: Total	Points/ Game	Assists	Steals	Blocked Shots	Rebounds: Total	Rebounds/ Game
1991	582	19.4	20	43	78	299	10
1992	632	20.4	46	56	54	261	8.4
1993	543	18.7	59	60	95	285	9.8
1994	657	21.9	83	69	94	369	12.3
TOTAL	2414	20.11	208	228	321	1214	10.1

OLYMPICS

Year	Points: Total	Points/ Game	Assists	Steals	Blocked Shots	Rebounds: Total	Rebounds/ Game
1996	n/a	19.5	n/a	n/a	n/a	n/a	7.3

WNBA

Year	Points: Total	Points/ Game	Assists (avg)	Steals	Blocked Shots	Rebounds: Total	Rebounds/ Game
1997	445	15.9	2.6	39	59	n/a	9.5

Lisa Leslie's Career Highlights

1989:
Member of the Junior World Championship team

1991:
Member of the gold medal–winning World University Games team
Named to the all-Pac-10 first team

1992:
Member of the gold medal–winning Jones Cup team
Named to the all-Pac-10 first team

1993:
USA Basketball Player of the Year as member of the World
  Championships qualifying team
Led USC in scoring and rebounding
Led Pac-10 in blocked shots
Named to the all-Pac-10 first team

1994:
Named to the all-Pac-10 first team (only player in Pac-10 history to
  receive this honor four times)
Named National Player of the Year
Led USC in scoring and rebounding
Led Pac-10 in blocked shots
Member of the gold medal–winning Goodwill Games team
Member of the bronze medal–winning World Championship team

1996:
Member of the gold medal–winning U.S. Olympic team
Member of the undefeated USA Basketball women's national team

1997:
Named to the all-WNBA first team

have to pass the test. She didn't want to make any more excuses.

She studied hard to make up for her educational shortcomings and took the test for the third time in April. She told a reporter she hoped that "the third time is the charm."

It was. This time, she scored 750. In early May she announced that she had decided to attend USC.

She was happy but apprehensive. "I'm glad I can play my freshman year," she said, "but the 750 is not as good as my own standards. To me, it's kind of terrible. Hopefully I won't be too far behind in college."

But with that kind of attitude, Lisa was already way ahead.

Chapter Seven:
1990–1994

A Whole New Ball Game

After spending the summer touring Canada with the U.S. junior team, Lisa began college in the fall of 1990. She quickly learned that being a collegiate athlete was much more demanding than being a high school basketball star. Back at Morningside, juggling schoolwork and sports had been easy. College was an entirely different story.

Basketball was only part of it. Her college classes were far more difficult than her high school classes had been, and Lisa had to study for several hours each day just to keep up. While attending college close to home had its advantages, it was also something of a distraction. Lisa had to resist the urge to go home every time she had a bad day as well as the constant temptation to forget about studying and just have fun. She tried to stay focused.

Chapter Seven:

1990–1994

A Whole New Ball Game

After spending the summer touring Canada with the U.S. junior team, Lisa began college in the fall of 1990. She quickly learned that being a collegiate athlete was much more demanding than being a high school basketball star. Back at Morningside, juggling schoolwork and sports had been easy. College was an entirely different story.

Basketball was only part of it. Her college classes were far more difficult than her high school classes had been, and Lisa had to study for several hours each day just to keep up. While attending college close to home had its advantages, it was also something of a distraction. Lisa had to resist the urge to go home every time she had a bad day as well as the constant temptation to forget about studying and just have fun. She tried to stay focused.

have to pass the test. She didn't want to make any more excuses.

She studied hard to make up for her educational shortcomings and took the test for the third time in April. She told a reporter she hoped that "the third time is the charm."

It was. This time, she scored 750. In early May she announced that she had decided to attend USC.

She was happy but apprehensive. "I'm glad I can play my freshman year," she said, "but the 750 is not as good as my own standards. To me, it's kind of terrible. Hopefully I won't be too far behind in college."

But with that kind of attitude, Lisa was already way ahead.

Playing basketball for Coach Marianne Stanley at USC demanded a greater commitment than Lisa had ever made before. Time was at a premium. Even before the season started, Lisa was expected to spend several hours every week working out. Then, when practices began in the fall of her freshman year, she had to find room in her daily schedule to accommodate them. The Lady Trojans played a national schedule and traveled back and forth across the country — so when the regular season started, Lisa discovered that she had to budget her time even more carefully. She hardly ever had a moment to herself!

At the same time, she was learning the hard facts about women's college sports. After all the attention she had gotten as a high school senior, it seemed as if hardly anyone paid much attention to her in college. At Morningside, most of her games had been sellouts. But at USC, as at most colleges, women's basketball wasn't nearly as big as men's basketball. The only women's games that were broadcast on television were the NCAA finals. USC's mediocre men's team played before thousands of spectators, while the women's team sometimes played for only a few hundred die-hard fans.

Women's collegiate basketball didn't get very much coverage in the newspapers, either. In fact, when Lisa was at Morningside, she received more press than she ever did at college. Despite the fact that under Coach Stanley the Lady Trojans women's basketball program was shaping up to be one of the best in the country, USC's female athletes were often treated like second-class citizens. Sometimes, it just didn't seem fair.

Lisa tried not to let any of these things bother her. She worked hard and tried to improve as a player and a person every day.

Coach Stanley named her a starting center as a freshman, and after only a few games, it was clear that she had been a wise choice. Lisa was a team leader. USC improved rapidly and challenged the opposition for the league title. They even qualified for the NCAA tournament.

Although USC lost in an early round, Lisa's freshman year had been a success. She averaged almost twenty points and ten rebounds per game. She was selected to the all-Pac-10 first team, an honor she would also receive in her sophomore, junior, and senior years, and was named both the Pac-10 and National Freshman of the Year. Had a male player earned the same honors, he would have appeared on magazine covers coast to coast. But apart from her teammates and opponents, few people knew who Lisa was.

Those who did know her knew enough to keep her playing. Her freshman year performance was impressive enough to allow her to continue to represent her country in the summer that followed it. She spent those months playing for the U.S. squad at the World University Games, where she averaged more than thirteen points and four rebounds per game.

In her second college season, USC won the Pac-10 championship, and she once again led USC into the NCAA tournament. This time they reached the quarterfinals before losing. Lisa was selected as a first-team All-American.

After the season ended, Lisa was invited to try out for the United States women's Olympic team, scheduled to play later that year at the summer games in Barcelona, Spain. At age nineteen, she was the youngest player invited to the tryouts.

But she didn't make the team. Although she was disappointed, she hadn't really expected to be selected. The other women were far more experienced than she was. Besides, if her game kept improving, she knew she would probably have a chance to make the team in 1996, when the Olympics were scheduled to play in Atlanta, Georgia. She was excited about the possibility of representing her country in front of American fans. In the meantime, there was still plenty of time to play ball.

In Lisa's third college season, USC was forced to rebuild after the graduation of several key players. Sometimes such rebuilding seasons can hurt a team. Yet due primarily to Lisa, the Lady Trojans again qualified for the NCAA tournament, and Lisa was named to the all-American team for the second consecutive season.

In the summer of 1993, Lisa again resumed her international career. She joined the U.S. national team and was named USA Basketball's Female Athlete of the Year. At the end of the summer, she returned to USC.

Yet just as her senior year was about to begin, Lisa and many of her teammates found themselves embroiled in the middle of a controversy. The dispute provided them with an invaluable — and painful — lesson in the relationship between men's and women's collegiate sports.

In the world of women's basketball, Coach Stanley was famous. One of the best coaches in the country, she had succeeded everywhere she had coached. Her record at USC proved that she had the ability to take a below-average team and make it great.

But despite her accomplishments, Coach Stanley wasn't paid nearly as much as USC men's basketball coach, George Raveling. Stanley didn't think that was fair and took her complaint to USC athletic director Mike Garrett, a former football star at the school. According to Stanley, Garrett promised her that in her next contract, she would be paid as much as Raveling.

Coach Stanley wasn't as concerned about the

money as she was about the concept of equality. She believed that since she was doing the same job as the men's coach, it was only fair — and right — that she be paid the same.

But when it came time to negotiate her next contract in June 1993, Stanley claimed that Garrett backed out on their deal. Upset, she went public with her complaint. Garrett claimed that in fact there had been no such agreement and that he had never planned on paying her as much as the men's coach.

In the off-season between Lisa's junior and senior year, the disagreement between Stanley and Garrett turned ugly. Just before school started in the fall of 1993, Stanley was fired. She responded by filing a sex discrimination suit against the university.

Lisa and the other members of the team were upset. They liked Coach Stanley and supported her. They didn't think it was fair that they had to have a new coach just because of a dispute over money.

As captain of the team, Lisa had a responsibility to her teammates. When several of them threatened to transfer from USC if Coach Stanley was not reinstated, Lisa decided she would transfer, too.

It was an important decision. According to NCAA rules, after players transfer, they have to sit out one full season before they would be eligible to play. But Lisa and her teammates were serious.

Yet after several weeks, it became clear to most of them, particularly the seniors, that it was probably too late to transfer. By the time they could enroll in another school, they'd have missed the beginning of the semester and it would be hard to catch up. In addition, they learned that their threat wouldn't bring back Coach Stanley. A new coach had already been hired. So in the end, they decided to stay and play as well as they possibly could.

The new coach was Cheryl Miller, the former USC star, widely considered to be the best women's college basketball player ever. Despite her reputation and her history with the college, the team didn't exactly warm to their new coach. They couldn't help feeling she had taken advantage of the situation by taking Stanley's job.

Still, they were a team and they had their pride. Before Stanley had left, there was talk that USC might win the Pac-10 title and challenge for the national championship. Now, after all the controversy and with all the adjustments they would have to make to a new coach, no one knew what to expect. No one, that is, except the Lady Trojans.

Led by Lisa, the team responded by playing great basketball. As Lisa told one reporter in reference to Miller, "You might not like your professor, but you still go to class." They opened with three straight tough road games and won all three to earn a top-twenty national ranking.

By mid-season, the team was 11–1 and ranked number nine. Lisa topped the two-thousand-point mark for her collegiate career with a thirty-one-point effort against Washington.

But after improving their record to 17–1 and reaching a number-four ranking, the Trojans stumbled and lost two straight games, including one to Stanford by thirty points. The loss cost them a shot at the Pac-10 title.

After the loss, Miller challenged the team to prove they were better than that and not lose another game all year. For a while, they succeeded and entered the NCAA tournament ranked eighth in the country and playing their best basketball of the season.

The tournament had expanded in 1994 to include sixty-four teams, twice as many as 1993. To win a national championship, the Trojans would have to win six tough games.

Just how challenging their uphill battle would be became clear when the tournament schedule was announced. USC was placed in the Mideast Region of the tournament. Of the sixteen teams in the region, four were ranked number eleven or higher. In order to reach the finals, the Trojans would have to play almost perfect basketball.

They almost did. After three victories, they still had to beat number-seven Louisiana Tech in the regional finals to advance to the Final Four. With twenty-three consecutive wins, Louisiana Tech was the hottest team in the country.

Although the Trojans played well and Lisa scored twenty-four points, the Trojans lost 75–66. Lisa's college career ended without a national championship.

In the post-season, Lisa felt a little better when she was chosen as an all-American for the third consecutive season and named the women's basketball Player of the Year. But that still didn't mean she was happy. "I would receive my awards in the mail to play in the Final Four," she admitted.

But it wasn't just missing out in the finals that made the end of her college career bittersweet. After years of playing basketball, she was suddenly faced with the prospect of being without a team. If she were a man, she would have known what the future held. A male player of her relative ability would be a certain number-one draft pick in the National Basketball Association and be offered a contract worth millions of dollars. But as a woman, she had no such opportunity.

"I think we're cheated as a gender," she told reporters after receiving the Player of the Year Award. "But there is nothing I can do about it except express my feeling about how unfair it is. It's unfortunate for all women's basketball players."

Now Lisa Leslie, perhaps the greatest player in the history of women's college basketball, had to make a decision.

What would she do next?

Chapter Eight:

1994–1995

Citizen of the World

Fortunately, Lisa graduated from college at just the right time. With the 1996 summer Olympic Games scheduled to be played in Atlanta, Georgia, women's basketball in the United States was on the upswing. USA Basketball, the governing body that manages both the men's and women's national teams, decided to reevaluate its women's basketball program. After the U.S. women's team won only a silver medal at the 1992 summer Olympics in Barcelona, they wanted to make certain that the team they sent to Atlanta was adequately prepared. The men's basketball gold-medal winning "Dream Team" of NBA stars in the 1992 Olympics had been a great success. USA Basketball wanted the women's team to be just as dominant.

In the summer of 1994, USA Basketball planned to select a team to play in the women's World Championship in Australia. Then, in May 1995, they would choose the U.S. national team. Although the Olympic team would not officially be selected until the summer of 1996, they expected its core to come from the national team. With corporate support that totaled three million dollars, the national players would be able to prepare for the Olympics for almost a year and even receive a small financial stipend so they could concentrate on basketball full-time.

At age twenty-one, Lisa wasn't ready to retire from basketball. She knew there was more for her to do on the basketball court. Making the national team was her opportunity to continue her career.

But it would be a full year before the national team would be created. In the meantime, Lisa had to find a way to keep playing basketball. She knew that if she stopped playing regularly, there was little chance she'd be prepared for the tryouts. So after graduating from USC, Lisa tried out for the World Championship team.

She made the team easily. The upcoming World Championship was an important tournament. Only those nations with the best teams at the World Championship would be invited to compete in Atlanta. Even though the United States received an automatic berth for being the host nation, the team wanted to make a statement at the World Championship — a statement that declared that the American women were the best basketball players in the world.

Lisa was the second youngest player on the team. Most of her teammates, like former Stanford star Jennifer Azzi and Texas Tech's Sheryl Swoopes, had already been out of college for several years. Guard Teresa Edwards, at age twenty-nine, was a veteran of three Olympic Games.

Yet Lisa was still one of the most talented players on the team. No other center in the history of American women's basketball had her unique set of skills. She had the size and strength of a center, the speed and jumping ability of a forward, and the ball-handling skills and shooting stats of a guard.

The tournament took place in Australia in early

June. The U.S. team got off to a quick start, blitzing South Korea 108–64. Then they dumped Spain, who had won the European title in 1993, 92–71, and crushed New Zealand 97–47.

The three victories qualified the United States for the quarterfinals and put them in medal contention. The remaining eight teams from the sixteen-team field would play to decide the championship.

Although they now faced better teams, the American women still knew how to win. They beat host Australia 88–70, then defeated Canada 98–65. In an exciting come-from-behind game, they edged out a rugged Slovakia squad 103–96 and advanced to the semifinals.

Lisa was having a great tournament. Sometimes when players have been stars, they have difficulty taking a back seat to play team basketball. On the World Championship team, most of the offense was designed around the team's talented and experienced forward, twenty-eight-year-old Katrina McClain. Lisa was supposed to play a supporting role.

She did so without complaint. Although she didn't lead the team in scoring in any one game, she was a consistent force in the middle — rebounding, playing defense, and scoring within the team's offensive concept.

The team entered the semifinals with a perfect 6–0 record. But now the Americans faced their toughest challenge: Brazil.

Even though the Brazilians had lost twice in the tournament, they were still alive in the hunt for the gold medal. They were a tough, experienced, athletic team. Their two stars, Silva Paula and Hortencia Oliveira, had played together for a decade and were as good as any two players in the world. The winning team of the U.S.–Brazil competition would play for the gold medal. The loser would have to play for the bronze.

The two teams were evenly matched, as the Americans' size and strength under the basket offset Brazil's superior outside game. In a close contest, neither team could pull away from the other. In the last minute of the game, Brazil held a slender lead. The United States was forced to foul to try to get the ball. But the Brazilians were perfect from the free-throw line. They made ten consecutive shots and eked out a 110–107 victory.

Lisa and her teammates were bitterly disappointed. They wanted to win the gold. Now they had to play a rematch against Australia for the bronze medal.

No one would have been surprised if the dejected American squad suffered a letdown and lost. But Lisa didn't let that happen.

Playing perhaps her best game of the tournament, she scored nineteen points as the United States held off a late run by their hosts to win 100–95. They won the bronze medal, but it wasn't the one they wanted. It was little comfort to know that the one team that had bested them, Brazil, eventually won the gold by defeating China. The women promised themselves that things would be different in Atlanta.

Lisa averaged more than ten points per game for the tournament and was second on the team in rebounds. She had performed well, but she realized that she had a lot of room for improvement. She was a good international player, but she wasn't great — not yet, anyway.

Although she had enjoyed her stint with the World Championship team, tryouts for the U.S. national team were still almost a year away. Lisa had to get a job and earn a living.

Ideally, she wanted to play basketball. But in the United States, that was impossible. There was no women's professional basketball league. After college, the active career of most female players ended.

That wasn't the case overseas. In several countries, women had played professionally in women's leagues for years. The Italian women's league was particularly strong. They recruited players from all over the world. Many of the women in the league also played for the national team of their native country. The competition was good, better than what Lisa had often faced in college.

She was contacted by a team sponsored by Sicilgesso, an Italian building products company, and offered a contract to play for their team based in Alcamo, Italy. Lisa jumped at the chance.

Although Lisa wasn't making a fortune, now she could look in the mirror every day and tell herself that she was a professional basketball player. She also knew the experience could help her reach her goal of playing in the Olympics. The Italian league played under international rules and gave Lisa the opportunity to become accustomed to the subtle differences of the international game.

The most obvious difference in basketball under international rules is the width of the free-throw lane. In the United States, the lane is sixteen feet wide from the sideline under the basket all the way to the free-throw line. Under international rules, the sixteen-foot free-throw lane splays out to become nineteen feet wide underneath the basket.

As a result, centers like Lisa can't set up quite so close to the basket. That results in a more wide-open game. Many teams depend more on good outside shooters than they do on a big tall center.

Lisa was far more mobile and athletic than most women who play center. The change actually helped her game, because it gave her more room to move and more opportunities to use her quickness and ball-handling skills. Despite being so tall, Lisa could handle the ball as well as many guards.

But that didn't mean Lisa had an easy time. Pro players play a much more physical game than Lisa was accustomed to. Players throw elbows, push and shove, and are just as rough as many men in the

NBA. Lisa had to adapt to this more aggressive style and learn to respond in kind. That didn't mean she learned to play dirty, but she did learn not to back off. If Lisa got pushed, sometimes she had to push back.

Her Italian team, made up of players from around the world, including several Americans, played only once or twice a week. That gave Lisa plenty of time to experience Italian culture. Although basketball had already taken her around the world, she had never had the time to really get to know what it was like to live in another country.

She enjoyed meeting Italians and learning the ways of their country. She traveled widely and visited the ancient yet cosmopolitan city of Rome several times. She even learned to speak some Italian.

She readily adapted to pro ball and became one of the best players in the league, averaging more than twenty points per game. Her team did well, too. Still, when the season ended early in the spring of 1995, Lisa knew she wasn't going to stay for a second season. She had another goal on her mind. A golden goal.

She returned home to Los Angeles and began to

look forward to tryouts for the national team. She played as much pickup basketball as possible, often against male college players. For as much as she had enjoyed playing in Italy, she much preferred playing at home. She looked forward to the opportunity to represent her own country again.

Chapter Nine:
1995–1996

Going National

National team tryouts were held in late May at the U.S. Olympic Training Center in Colorado Springs, Colorado. Tara VanDerveer was head coach of the team.

Lisa Leslie was no surprise to Coach VanDerveer. She had coached Lisa on several national teams in the past, including the World Championship team. She was also the coach at Stanford University, USC's arch rival in the Pac-10. She was taking the year off from Stanford to coach the national team.

But even though Coach VanDerveer knew Lisa was a great player, that didn't mean that Lisa was automatically a member of the team. For the first time, American women basketball players were going to be paid to represent their country and play the sport they loved. Everyone wanted to be a member of this groundbreaking group. New college graduates were anxious to make their mark. There were also a number of veterans who had just failed to make the World Championship team and had been working hard and practicing ever since, including some players who had played overseas, as Lisa had.

More than sixty women were invited to participate in the grueling seven-day tryout. Only eleven players would make the team, although several others would be allowed to try out again during the upcoming year. The final Olympic squad wouldn't be announced until the following summer.

Lisa's hard work in Italy and in the gyms around Los Angeles paid off. She made the team! The Americans immediately departed for Europe to play a series of scrimmages. They then recessed for the summer, before coming together again in Colorado Springs in October.

They were the most talented group of American women basketball players ever assembled. Already, some observers were calling them the women's "Dream Team" and the best team in the world.

They were a fine mix of experienced veterans

such as guard Teresa Edwards and forward Katrina McClain and emerging young stars such as Lisa and guard Sheryl Swoopes, who had scored forty-seven points in the NCAA championship game during her senior year in college. One big addition was the University of Connecticut's center, Rebecca Lobo, who was fresh from leading UConn to the NCAA title.

But the women knew that having talented individuals on the team wasn't going to be enough to win — the World Championship had proven that. In order to win, the Americans had to learn to play together as a team.

When the team got together again in October, they practiced for several weeks. Coach VanDerveer taught the players her style of basketball, which featured a pressure defense and a fast-breaking offense. Then the team embarked on an ambitious fifty-two-game "world tour," primarily playing against American college teams in the United States, as well as facing national and club teams overseas. The purpose of the tour was twofold.

By playing so many games, the Americans hoped to build the team unity that is so important for a winning effort. Previous American teams had always been hampered by the fact that they usually had to compete within only a month or two of playing together for the first time.

The second reason was to raise the profile of women's basketball in the United States. By playing all over the country, they hoped to expose women's basketball to fans who had never paid attention to the women's game before.

They opened play on October 28, 1995, in Cincinnati, Ohio, against the Athletes in Action, a semipro team that uses basketball to help spread their religious message. They were a tough, experienced team that competed equally with the best collegiate teams in the country. Everyone expected the Athletes in Action to give the national team a good game.

Wrong! The American women swamped AIA before eighteen hundred fans, 83–57. Lisa Leslie scored twenty-four points to lead all scorers.

Compared to her experience in the World Championship the previous summer, Lisa was now a much more important part of the United States' offense. Her experience in Italy and subsequent hard work had paid off. Her athleticism, combined with her newfound aggressiveness, made her nearly un-stoppable. She was equally adept at posting up down low, finishing off the fast break, or playing on the perimeter. She began to dominate the game just as she so often had in college.

The team tore through their twenty-one-game schedule against college teams, going undefeated. They even dumped the defending NCAA champion Connecticut Huskies by the resounding score of 83–47. Their only "close" game was a twenty-eight-point win over Vanderbilt. In the final game of the collegiate tour, they beat Colorado 107–24. On aver-age, they defeated their college opponents by forty-five points!

Many of the sportswriters who covered the games had expected to smirk at the women's play. Instead, they came away impressed. They began to realize that these women weren't just good women's bas-ketball players. They were good players, period. Be-cause women are not as tall as men, the game highlighted skill and strategy rather than strength. Yet they were surprised to discover that Lisa could post up under the basket and use the same moves that men did in the NBA, and that Sheryl Swoopes could penetrate to the basket and then dish off just like an NBA point guard. The team played zone defense, blocked shots, and ran fast breaks, just as the men did.

Fans were similarly astonished. They couldn't believe how good the women were. For the first time, many fans realized that women didn't play some lesser game called "women's basketball." They played basketball, and it was just as much fun to watch talented women play as it was to watch men.

In January 1996, the team traveled to Russia and Ukraine, where they won eight more times against Russia's best club team and the Ukrainian national team. Then in March they traveled to China for the International Challenge Tournament, a warm-up for the Olympics. Scheduled to play eight games in eight days, the Americans would be facing a tough test. The Chinese team featured their massive center Zheng Haixia, who at six-foot-eight was the tallest woman in basketball. She was known as the "Great Wall of China."

But the U.S. passed the test with flying colors, winning all eight games despite missing several injured players. Lisa had little trouble with Zheng. She was just too quick for the Great Wall.

In May the team traveled to Australia for another tournament. They remained undefeated.

Their exhibition schedule wrapped up in May and June with a series of six games in the United States and Canada against Cuba, Canada, and Russia.

In their next-to-the-last game, against Russia in Chicago on June 15, they got a wake-up call. While looking ahead to the Olympics, they almost lost a tough contest to the Russian team. Although the Americans squeaked by with a 80–79 win, not paying attention to the game at hand almost cost them their unofficial title as international champs.

Now the tour was over. The team had gone undefeated. Lisa had paced the squad with an average of over 17 points and 7 rebounds per game. As an example of her improving game, she even made 12 of 31 three-point shots, the second best percentage on the team.

The grueling exhibition schedule had served its purpose. The Americans had learned to play together as a team and had raised the profile of women's basketball in the United States. Their tour drew more than one-quarter of a million fans, a number no one would have believed possible only a year or two before.

Lisa and her teammates were becoming famous. Lisa's attractive face and slender frame especially stood out. She was approached by the media and soon appeared on the cover of both *Sports Illustrated* and the fashion magazine *Vogue*. She enjoyed modeling and hoped to do more of it after the Olympics.

Lisa, Sheryl Swoopes, and Dawn Staley even appeared in a television commercial for sneakers directed by note filmmaker Spike Lee. In the commercial, Lisa and her teammates play ball against men at an outdoor playground. Only a few months before, that idea would have been laughable. But no one laughed now. Everyone was beginning to realize that women could really play.

Lisa Leslie would soon prove just that to the entire world.

Chapter Ten:
1996

A Golden Moment

The Olympic Games opened in Atlanta on July 21, 1996. Lisa was thrilled as she walked into the stadium with the other members of the United States Olympic team and watched as Muhammad Ali lit the Olympic torch, signifying the beginning of the games. Then she knew it was time to work.

Before their first game, Coach VanDerveer gave each woman on the team a set of goals, both for herself and for the team. But Lisa added a few that didn't have much to do with the game on the court.

During the long international tour, she had begun to realize that she had a role larger than basketball. Little girls looked up to her. She began to receive dozens of fan letters every day. She made a point of trying to inspire the girls in the right direction.

"When I go out there to play the game, I'm going to be aggressive," she told a reporter, "but when the game's over, I'm going to come out and be a lady. I think it's important for little girls to see you don't have wear your clothes all baggy and have your pants hanging down and your hat on backwards to play basketball." Lisa wanted the girls to realize that women could play basketball in their own right. They didn't have to look or act like boys.

The U.S. opened against Cuba. Although the national team had defeated Cuba five times, several of the games had been close. The Americans knew it wasn't going to be an easy game.

The tiny gym at Morehouse College, site of the first round of competition, was almost full. President Clinton's daughter, Chelsea, was in the stands, as were NBA stars Magic Johnson and Scottie Pippen. The American women couldn't believe it.

They started off nervous and played tentatively, as if they were afraid of losing. Of course, when you play like that, losing is often what happens.

Cuba jumped out to an early lead. Coach VanDerveer went to her bench early.

Halfway through the first half, Lisa went scrambling for a loose ball. As she bent over, a Cuban player inadvertently kneed her in the head. She went down hard.

Stunned, she stayed on the ground for a few moments before slowly rising to her feet. Coach VanDerveer removed her from the game. Lisa could only watch helplessly from the sidelines as her teammates struggled to stay on top.

At halftime, Lisa told the coach she felt well enough to play. The team doctor told her it was okay.

When Lisa returned to the lineup, it seemed to fire up the team. Soon after the halftime buzzer, the Americans took command. Lisa finished with twenty-four points, and the U.S. won, 101–84.

In game two, the Americans faced Ukraine. This time Lisa made sure they got off to a quick start.

Lisa jumped center for the American team. When the referee threw the ball into the air, she leaped up and tipped it to teammate Sheryl Swoopes. Then she raced down-court.

Swoopes didn't waste time. She pushed the ball up-court and hit Lisa on the run with a bullet pass.

Lisa gathered the ball in, soared through the air, and laid it into the hoop. She was fouled on the play and sank the free throw. With the game less than five seconds old, the U.S. led, 3–0.

The quick start set the tone for the game. Keyed by Lisa's rebounding and defense, the U.S. team kept beating the Ukrainians down-court on the fast break. The Americans romped to a 98–65 win.

For its third game, against Zaire, the team was scheduled to play at the Georgia Dome, where the men's NBA "Dream Team" also played. When the American women ran out on the court to start their warm-ups, they couldn't believe their eyes.

The huge building was packed floor to ceiling with fans, who cheered and roared and waved flags and banners. Over thirty thousand spectators filled the stands, the largest crowd to ever see a women's basketball game.

From the opening tip, the American women gave a basketball clinic. Crisp passing, deadly shooting, and swarming defense marked their play against overmatched Zaire. The U.S. won easily, 107–47.

After the game, the women stayed in the locker room, basking in the glow of the game. Lisa summed it up perfectly: "A lot of people may have seen women's basketball for the first time today and said, 'Wow!'"

She was right. Along with the equally surprising and successful U.S. women's soccer team, the women's "Dream Team" became the story of the Olympics. The men's team, while winning easily, didn't appear to be playing very hard or having much fun. In contrast, the women were exciting and dynamic.

Two more wins in front of capacity crowds qualified the United States for the medal round. They were playing well, but now they had to do so under increasing pressure. The entire world was watching and expecting them to win.

They faced Japan in the opening game of the medal round. Although no one on the Japanese roster was over six feet tall, they were deadly shooters from the outside.

For the U.S. to succeed, Lisa had to take advantage of the smaller Japanese frontcourt. She made it look easy. Time after time, her teammates got her the ball, and time after time, Lisa went to the basket, spinning around the opposition or simply soaring over them. She scored an Olympic record thirty-five points to pace the U.S. to a 108–93 win.

"I didn't realize I was on," she said afterward. "My teammates did a great job of getting me the ball, and when I get the ball, I try to put it in the basket or make the best decision." That day, no one questioned Lisa's decisions.

The victory put the United States into the semifinals against Australia. In the other semifinal contest, Brazil played China. So far, the Olympics were playing out a lot like the World Championship.

But the night before the game, the Olympics were rocked by a bomb blast at Olympic Park. When the explosive went off, the team was asleep at its hotel only a few blocks away.

The explosion woke everyone. For the rest of the night the women huddled around the television, watching coverage of the blast's aftermath.

That was hardly the way they wanted to spend the night before the most important game of their lives. But they were determined not to let the bombing keep them from their goal. In fact, they felt that it was their responsibility to prove to the world that the bombing was an aberration. They wanted to show everyone that the spirit of the Olympics couldn't be stopped. They took to the court ready to play a show-stopping game.

After a slow start, veteran Teresa Edwards followed Lisa's remarkable performance against the Japanese with one of her own. No one on the Australian team could keep up with her. She scored 20 points, dished out 15 assists, and even grabbed 7 rebounds. Her spectacular play keyed an American run following a 56–56 tie score that put the game away. The United States won, 96–79.

Meanwhile, Brazil beat China 81–60. The U.S. team was excited about the rematch. After losing to Brazil at the World Championship, the Americans all felt they had something to prove.

"That one game did more for America's women's basketball than anything," said Coach VanDerveer in a press conference before the gold medal game, referring to the team's loss against Brazil in the World Championship. "That game is the reason we've had this team together for a year."

Added Lisa Leslie, "After that loss, I always

visualized playing Brazil again." Then Teresa Edwards spoke for everyone on the team. "What are we out here for," she said, "if we don't win a gold medal?"

Entering the contest, both teams were undefeated. And unlike the other teams the Americans had played, the Brazilians were confident. They didn't just hope they'd win; they knew they could. They promised to provide the Americans with their stiffest competition of the Olympic Games.

The game took place on the final night of the Olympics, the last scheduled event. More than thirty-two thousand fans poured into the Georgia Dome while millions more tuned in on television all around the world. For that one night at least, women's basketball was the only game in town.

As in their first game of the Olympics, the American women got off to a slow start. The confident Brazilians took full advantage of the U.S. team's tentative play.

The Americans began the game playing woman-to-woman defense, believing that their superior backcourt speed would help shut down Silva Paula and Hortencia Oliveira. It did, but Brazil was not just a two-woman team.

In the opening minutes of the game, Brazil's six-foot-two center, Marta De Sooza Sobral, proved that she could match Lisa Leslie in speed and agility. Every time Lisa slid over to help out another player on defense, Sobral sliced toward the basket and her alert teammates got her the ball. Too often, Lisa was just a split second too late to keep Sobral away from the basket. In the game's first eight minutes, Sobral scored eleven points. Lisa, meanwhile, was scoreless.

But Sobral paid a penalty for her aggressiveness. Although she was effective, she was playing a little out of control. Halfway through the first half, she picked up her third foul.

She now had to play more cautiously, particularly on defense. That gave Lisa a chance to regroup. She didn't let the opportunity get away from her.

The Americans clawed back to take a slim 27–24 lead, then rebounded a missed shot by Brazil and worked the ball down-court. Hampered by her third foul, Sobral was no match for Lisa. Lisa posted up, got the ball, and put it into the hoop. Her first basket gave the U.S. a 29–24 lead.

The Brazilian coach was quick to respond. Sobral was pulled from the game.

Lisa's teammates quickly realized that Brazil's second-string center couldn't keep up with her. They kept putting the ball into Lisa's hands.

Just as she had made good decisions and put it into the basket against Japan earlier in the tournament, she did so again. She kept slicing toward the hoop for easy shots.

Lisa keyed a 14–7 run that ended when she scored a basket and a free throw for a three-point play to put the U.S. ahead, 41–31. At the half, the United States still led by eleven, at 57–46. After going scoreless over the game's first ten minutes, Lisa finished the half with fifteen points.

At halftime, Coach VanDerveer told her team to keep playing hard and take the game to the Brazilians. She needn't have worried.

On Brazil's first possession of the second half, American guard Ruthie Bolten stripped the ball from Silva Paula. Anticipating the play, Sheryl Swoopes raced down-court. Bolten passed her the ball. Swoopes scored on an uncontested layup.

Brazil got the ball back and again tried to score. Oliveira tried a jumper but missed. The rebound went long over Lisa's outstretched hands, but Bolten was in the right position. She grabbed the ball and spotted Katrina McClain racing toward the American basket. She made another great pass that McClain converted to a layup to put the U.S. ahead 61–46.

Brazil inbounded the ball, but Sheryl Swoopes challenged Brazilian Janeth Arcain and stole it. Brazil called a timeout to try to stem the American tide.

The crowd roared with delight as the two teams returned to their benches. Up in the stands, someone was waving a banner back and forth that read *This is the real Dream Team!* The chant of "U.S.A.! U.S.A.!" echoed through the arena.

The Americans put the ball in play underneath their own basket. As the Brazilian defense collapsed on Lisa to prevent a lob pass, McClain saw an opening and charged to the basket. The lob pass came to her, and the U.S. scored again to make the score 63–46.

Once more, Brazil tried to work the ball in for a basket to stop the Americans' scoring streak. But Lisa was in perfect position under the basket.

A shot went up, but so did Lisa. At the peak of her

leap, she swatted the ball out of the air to one of her teammates, then raced down-court.

She set up along the baseline and waved for the ball. She got it, spun to the hoop, and powered the ball through.

In only two minutes, the Americans had turned the close game into a rout. Now the scoreboard read *U.S.A. 65, Brazil 46.* The roaring and chanting from the crowd increased. The celebration had begun.

Brazil was powerless to stop the Americans. Everyone on the U.S. team was hot. They continued to frustrate Brazil's backcourt. Brazil's only chance to get back into the game was to shoot three-pointers, but the American guards dogged their Brazilian counterparts on every shot. When the Brazilian guards did get a shot off, they were stone cold — and Lisa was under the basket, picking off the rebound and starting another fast break.

Everyone on the United States team got into the game and scored. When the final buzzer sounded, the entire team raced onto the court, hugging one another and crying tears of joy. The final score was the United States 111, Brazil 87.

The Americans had shot an astounding 66 percent from the field. Lisa led all scorers with 29 points on 5 free throws and 12-of-14 shooting from the field. Over the course of the Olympics, she averaged 28.7 points per game and made nearly three-quarters of her shots. Then, in front of a worldwide audience, she and her teammates had made the strongest possible case for the future of women's basketball. No one could say they didn't know how to play the game and play it well.

The entire Georgia Dome turned into the site of an impromptu party as nearly everyone stayed for the medal ceremony. As Lisa stood on the podium with her teammates and sang the "Star-Spangled Banner" with a chorus of more than thirty thousand fans in accompaniment, she fingered the gold medal that now hung around her neck.

She had never seen anything so beautiful or felt so proud.

Chapter Eleven:
1996-1997

A League of Their Own

At a press conference after the game, Lisa and her teammates were ecstatic. "These are women who worked really hard," said Coach VanDerveer. "We were on a mission all year. They took care of business."

"It's been very difficult," Lisa agreed, "but to beat anything in life, it takes team discipline. All I can say is 'No pain, no gain.'

"This is the best moment of my life," she added. "We're leaving Atlanta as gold medalists."

But Lisa had precious little time to bask in the glory of the moment. Before the press conference ended, she was peppered with questions about her future. Eighteen months earlier, she wouldn't have had much of an answer for those questions. But all of a sudden, her world was full of opportunities.

The Olympics had made her a star. The team's efforts through the year had raised America's awareness of women's basketball. Two American women's professional leagues were in the works: the American Basketball League, or ABL, and the Women's Professional Basketball Association, or WNBA. Since Lisa was now one of the most famous and talented women players in the world, each league was certain to go after her and try to convince her to play for them. Overseas leagues were also certain to try to bid for her services.

But at the same time, her appearances in commercials and on magazine covers had not gone unnoticed in the world of high-fashion modeling. Lisa's striking good looks, long slender body, effervescent personality, and celebrity status made her attractive to advertisers and fashion designers. Just before the Olympics, she had signed a contract with the prestigious Wilhelmina modeling agency. She loved wearing fancy clothes and being the center of attention. Modeling reminded her of when she was a child and her mother would hold fashion shows in her living room.

Fortunately, she didn't have to decide upon either

basketball or modeling right away. The pro leagues were still in the planning stages. She told the press, "I plan to model first, but I'm sure I'll play the game again. I'm just not sure about when or where."

As for the present, "I'm just tired," she admitted. "I've been playing basketball nonstop for ten years," ever since her cousin Craig had dragged her to the gym for the first time.

But she was certain about one thing. She wanted to continue fulfilling her responsibility to her young fans. "Over the next five years," she said, "I'd definitely like some little girl to look at me as someone who's a woman — intelligent, attractive — and an athlete. I like my image, and hope it remains the same, as a basketball player and a model."

In the months after the Olympics, Lisa pursued her modeling career. But as she had suspected, she couldn't stop playing basketball. She loved the game too much.

The ABL got underway first, in the fall of 1996, and announced that their season would last until the spring. Then the WNBA announced that they would begin play with a twenty-eight-game summer schedule.

Some observers worried that both leagues wouldn't be able to survive and that eventually only one would remain. The players each league would be able to recruit might well be the determining factor in its survival.

Both leagues wanted Lisa. But although each was a pro league, there were subtle differences.

The ABL was an independent league, while the WNBA was affiliated with the NBA. The ABL had decided to play with the men's basketball, while the WNBA chose to use the women's collegiate ball, which is one inch smaller in circumference. Due to its affiliation with the NBA, the WNBA was able to secure a television contract spread over NBC, ESPN, and Lifetime. The ABL television contract was much smaller.

Then there was the question of money. On average, the ABL paid players a higher salary. But the WNBA was in a better position to pay high-profile players like Lisa even more.

While some of her Olympic teammates chose to start playing right away and joined the ABL, Lisa decided to wait and signed with the WNBA. She felt that the future of the WNBA was more secure and provided larger commercial opportunities for her. They also offered her a better contract and a chance to play at home, with the league's Los Angeles franchise, the Sparks.

In the months before the season started, Lisa focused on her modeling career. She stayed in shape by working out at USC and with a personal trainer. She also acted as a spokesperson for the WNBA. She kept telling everyone not to forget about the Olympics. "When you come watch a women's basketball game," she said, "you'll keep coming back for more."

The league opened play on June 22, 1997, when the Sparks entertained the New York Liberty at the Los Angeles Forum, the same arena used by the NBA's Los Angeles Lakers. More than fourteen thousand fans turned out to watch.

The game featured Lisa and the WNBA's other high-profile star, the Liberty's Rebecca Lobo. It was broadcast to a national television audience.

Lisa knew that the opening games of the fledgling league could make a big difference on how the rest of the season was perceived. She wanted to do her part — and the best thing she could think to do was to dunk during the game. She had often done so in high school but had steered away from the shot while playing on the Olympic team. While she could make the shot easily, she was a little afraid about being inadvertently undercut by another player and getting hurt. But she knew that a dunk shot in the first game would bring the league a lot of attention.

Lisa jumped center for the Sparks to open the game. When she tipped to teammate Jamila Wideman, she became the first player in WNBA history to touch the ball. A few minutes later, the perfect opportunity to dunk appeared. Lisa broke loose on a fast break, and there was no one between her and the basket.

But she got too excited. By the time she jumped, she was too far beneath the basket and missed the shot. Fortunately, a teammate put the ball back in the hoop.

Both teams showed their nerves and played cautiously in the inaugural contest. New York opened up a lead with an 8–0 first-half run and held on to win, 67–57. Lisa tied for the game-high with sixteen points and pulled down fourteen rebounds.

Despite the loss and her missed dunk, Lisa was delighted by just having the opportunity to play again. "We were pretty overwhelmed by the crowd," she admitted afterward. "But the level of play is going to improve. The best thing I can compare this to is our U.S. national team. You did not see us playing after one month of practice. We just weren't in synch. It's going to take a little time to get ourselves together."

Lisa was right. In their next game, the Sparks combined with Utah to score 191 points. Even though the Sparks lost, they were slowly improving.

Lisa was the one consistent player on the team over the first month, usually leading her teammates in scoring. And while the Sparks were rarely blown out, they lost a number of games that they could have won.

When the Sparks record fell to 4–7 after a loss to Sacramento on July 15, coach Linda Sharp was fired and replaced by Julie Rousseau. After their record slumped to 5–10, she made some lineup changes, and soon the Sparks began playing better.

They became less dependent on Lisa to provide scoring punch and began to play better team basketball. Teammate Zheng Haixia, the "Great Wall of China," improved, and Tamecka Dixon and Penny

Toler emerged as two of the most consistent scorers in the league.

The season's highlight was a game in Cleveland against the Rockers on August 7. The Sparks were coming off a big win over New York. With a record of 9–12, both the Sparks and Cleveland, at 11–9, were still in the running for their division championship and a spot in the post-season playoffs. The Rockers were hot and had won their last eight of nine games.

After regulation play, the score was tied 68–68. The game entered overtime.

But at the end of that period, the score was still tied, 74–74. The two teams were forced to play a second five-minute period.

With L.A. nursing a 76–75 lead and three minutes remaining, Lisa got the ball on the perimeter. The Rocker defense didn't bother coming out to her.

She made them pay and drilled a long jump shot for a three-pointer to put the Sparks ahead 79–75. Cleveland tried to get back into the game, but with only a few seconds left, Lisa outmaneuvered a Cleveland player for a rebound after Zheng missed a free throw. That sealed the win.

"As a player, you dream about going into overtime or double overtime," she said. "We really needed this win."

Over the last month of the season, the Sparks played some of the best basketball in the WNBA. On August 18, they played the division-leading Phoenix Mercury. In order to even have a chance at the division title, the Sparks had to win this game.

Lisa was extra-motivated, because Cheryl Miller, Lisa's former coach at USC, coached Phoenix.

She responded by playing one of her best games of the year. She dominated Phoenix center Jennifer Gillom, scoring twenty-six points and collecting fifteen rebounds as the Sparks won, 75–66. With only three games remaining in the season, the Sparks, at 12–13, trailed Phoenix by only one game.

In the end, it all came down to the final game of the season. The Sparks had won their last two games, putting their record at 14–13. They faced the Mercury again — and if the Sparks won, the two teams would tie for the title. But because the Sparks already had the best record in head-to-head competition between the two teams, L.A. would be declared division champions and win the right to face eastern conference champion Houston in the first-ever WNBA finals.

At halftime, Phoenix led 29–22. If the Sparks hoped to win, they had to get going.

The Mercury collapsed around Lisa down low, so it was up to guards Tamecka Dixon and Penny Toler to get the Sparks back in the game. With less than a minute left to play, the score was tied 64–64.

L.A. had the ball out of bounds. Lisa prepared to throw it in. The Sparks planned to run the clock down and try for the final shot.

She spotted Dixon wide open and passed the ball in her direction. But Phoenix's Umeki Webb anticipated the pass and came out of nowhere to steal the ball!

Lisa was crushed, but she had to quickly forget about it and get back on defense.

Now the Mercury maneuvered for the last shot. With time running out, Jennifer Gillom got the ball.

Although Gillom had already scored twenty-seven points, it had taken her twenty-five shots to make them. Lisa had made her work — and she wasn't about to let up now.

Gillom tried a shot from eighteen feet. Lisa was in

her face the whole way. The ball rattled around the rim and fell out as time expired. Overtime!

But in the extra period, Los Angeles ran out of steam. The Mercury jumped ahead on a three-pointer, and the Sparks just couldn't catch up. Phoenix won, 73–68, to capture the western division title and qualify for the finals, which they eventually lost to Houston.

Lisa Leslie was disappointed but philosophical after the loss. She was proud of the way the team played after their poor start. "We just did what we could to try to come through an adverse situation," she said in regard to the Sparks' problems earlier in the season. "But we did our best."

Lisa was named to the all-WNBA first team, as she led the league in rebounds, was second in blocks, and third in points, with a 16.4 average. It was a good beginning, but she knew she could do better. After all, that's what she'd done ever since she had stepped on a basketball court for the first time.

She looked forward to the future and was keenly aware of her role as a pioneer in women's professional basketball.

"I always try to make sure I sign little boys' autographs," she once told a reporter. "Twenty years from now, if one of them is a guy making the corporate decision, I want him to say, 'Why shouldn't I give a woman the opportunity to play pro sports?'"

The girl who once hated basketball had come a long, long way.

All available in paperback from Little, Brown and Company

Matt Christopher

Sports Bio Bookshelf

Andre Agassi

Wayne Gretzky

Ken Griffey Jr.

Mia Hamm

Grant Hill

Randy Johnson

Michael Jordan

Lisa Leslie

Greg Maddux

Hakeem Olajuwon

Emmitt Smith

Mo Vaughn

Tiger Woods

Steve Young

MATT CHRISTOPHER

On the Court with...

Lisa Leslie

Little, Brown and Company

Boston   New York   Toronto   London